LEADERSHIP
WITH LESS STRESS

How to increase productivity and happiness
in your leadership and workplace.

AskDrAnnika

Less stressed leaders mean less stressed employees!

Learn Stress Management Skills

Be Energized and Avoid Anxiety

Be Inspired and Increase Profit

Dr Annika Sörensen is an M.D., Author, International Motivational Speaker and Stress Management Coach. As Seen on:

Empower your management teams with a stress management toolkit.

Book Dr Annika for an in house Full Day/Half Day Workshop, Motivational Speaking or Over Dinner Talk on:

> From Stressed Out, Maxed Out and Burned Out to Calm

> Happiness In The Work Environment

> Leadership and Communication

Or have a talk or workshop tailored to your own company.

"Thank you so much for a most excellent speech in Malmö. Dr Annika, you were so good and I just devoured everything you said. Today my shoulders automatically sink when I think of you – I find that amusing. You are so generous with your knowledge, a very wise woman. I am so glad I got a chance to listen to you." ~ C Ahlström

 annika@askdrannika.com

 askdrannika.com

TAKE
stress
FROM
chaos
TO calm

**Pulling the Pieces Together:
How to Find Your Best Self,
Re-Energize and Participate in Life**

DR. ANNIKA SÖRENSEN

LIONCREST

Take Stress from Chaos to Calm
Pulling the Pieces Together: How to Find Your Best Self, Re-Energize and Participate in Life

For information about this title or to order other books and/or electronic media, contact the publisher:

Dr. Annika
annika@askdrannika.com
https://www.askdrannika.com

ISBN: 978-1-62865-085-3

"First, say to yourself what would you be: then do what you have to do."

— *Epictetus*

Table of Contents

Foreword   vii

Introduction   ix

CHAPTER 1: Self-Development – The Man in the Mirror   1

CHAPTER 2: Health: You Can't Live Without It   11

CHAPTER 3: Happiness at Work: Can You Feel It?   43

CHAPTER 4: How Important is Money?   49

CHAPTER 5: Can You Relate?   55

CHAPTER 6: Come a Little Closer   61

CHAPTER 7: Free Time Rests Your Brain!   67

CHAPTER 8: Where Do You Belong?   73

Summary   79

APPENDIX A: Sleep Diary   81

APPENDIX B: Diet Diary   83

APPENDIX C: Physical Activity Diary   85

APPENDIX D: Stress Journal   87

APPENDIX E: "Important/Urgent Tool"   89

APPENDIX F: Plus-Minus List   91

APPENDIX G: Work Environment Policy   93

APPENDIX H: Cash Flow Chart   95

APPENDIX I: Annual Budget   97

APPENDIX J: Intimacy Inventory   99

APPENDIX K: Pros and Cons List   101

Foreword

"When people are ready to, they change. They never do it before then, and sometimes they die before they get around to it. You can't make them change if they don't want to, just like when they do want to, you can't stop them."

—*Andy Warhol,* Andy Warhol: In His Own Words

THERE'S A PRICE TO PAY to be at the top. You've heard this before, but have you ever considered what this really means?

I've seen it many times — entrepreneurs and ambitious business people who don't quite make it all the way. These people are exhausted from doing everything they think they have to do, and they've forgotten the basis of all prosperous life/businesses — taking good care of themselves. They've become their own worst enemy.

As a business leader you're probably conducting your own juggling act — multi-tasking, managing too many things at once — with many who rely on your input and expertise. If you're like most, you probably have a hand in every aspect of your business — from advertising, booking, sales, your network — in addition to your personal and family relationships.

But Who Takes Care of You?

With all the responsibilities you have, it's easy to forget yourself — your own health — until it's too late.

If this sounds familiar, this book is for you. It will help you take the first step toward a healthy and fulfilling life.

This content is good for everyone. The goal is to make things as easy as possible. No difficult or expensive methods you have to commit to — just commit to yourself and take the steps one by one. Some of it will be easy, and some of it will be challenging. Self-work can be hard because you're dealing with your thoughts, your feelings and your body. (Although rare, if you start to feel anxious or scared, I recommend you seek professional help by your doctor or by a live coach.)

You spend so much time at work, and give so much to so many during your work-years — let them be happy, fun, meaningful, energetic, and healthy. Do this, and you'll do wonders in your work/ company — and who knows, you might even change the world.

Introduction

"You'll never leave where you are until you decide where you want to be."

— *Unknown*

I T'S EASY to take good care of yourself, right? We're all "self-made" people. We have what it takes and we know what to do. With all the information out there on balance — how to work right, eat right, sleep right, love right, think right, walk right, talk right, exercise right . . . and the list goes on. We're all doing it right, right?

If so, then why are so many people depressed, stressed, in conflict in relationship, at work, even at play?

I think we've got it wrong. We talk about how much we've evolved over time, and in part, it's true. But for human beings to really be functional, satisfied — truly happy — I think we need to go back to the basics. Our brains seek stimulation, and our bodies need to move! Period. And we have to find models to help keep us on that track.

It's been said, that "All roads lead to Rome." I think this applies to regaining control of our lives as well. There are many ways to re-energize and fully participate in our own lives on all levels. My method is clear and simple: commit to our "whole being," and recapture our inner power which helps us navigate the turnstiles of life.

We must dare to be true to ourselves — to see ourselves as we really are, and then commit to who we know we want to be, and can most definitely be. We must dare to seek the "man in the mirror," to truly understand we can't change anyone but ourselves. It's when we truly accept this notion, that we can make positive changes for the future.

"The Wheel of Life"

So how do you become the happy, healthy, prosperous leader you always dreamed you'd be?

And what's the easiest way to get there? By recognizing the fact that you are a complex being. Together, you and I can identify what drives you as a person — physically, mentally, and spiritually.

I'll show you how to tackle the issues you're facing, and help you find a more holistic way of living. The eight-piece model I use is called the "Wheel of Life," and it represents key areas, which together define you and illustrate everything that matters in your life.

The pieces are:

1. **Personal Development** — Who are you? You need to really get to know yourself to be able to know what you need and where you want to go. This includes mind, body, and spirit. It's about identity. Knowing yourself also makes it easier to relate and communicate with your fellow human beings.
2. **Health** — Where are you on the health scale? How do you take care of yourself? This piece of the pie is divided into 5 sub pieces (sleep, diet, physical activity, stress and stimulators) to cover all issues. By the way, this piece is critical. In fact, I would say it's the foundation for everything.

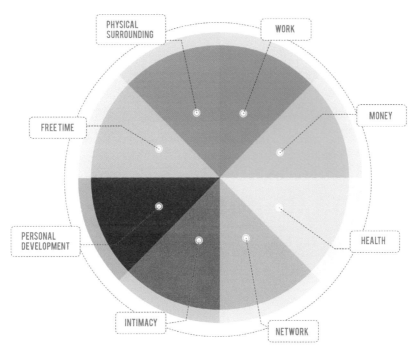

The Wheel of Life

3. **Work** — You spend at least half your awake time at work —
   most likely more. You need to find happiness in your work to
   make it worthwhile and to make a difference for yourself, the
   company and your costumers. Surprise! This also increases
   profitability.

4. **Money** — Money is not just about numbers, it's also a lot
   about feelings. These underlying feelings may complicate
   our action in ways we don't see if we don't bring them to
   the surface. Gaining control about your current financial
   situation, as well as your attitudes about money will make
   a huge difference.

5. **Network** — We are pack animals. Having good, healthy networks will help you get the most out of your life — at work,

at home, in your community, and in the world, at large. Is your networking currently working for your good?

6. **Intimacy** — Without close human contacts your heart and soul will shrink. This is about the most basic of needs for a thriving life. If you are not seen for the good things you are and do you will seek attention in a negative way. This is about self-esteem.

7. **Free time/hobbies** — Work is important, but it doesn't define us entirely. Most leaders don't have too much free time, which makes it even more important that what you do in your free time helps your body, mind and soul rest. It's also about finding the little things in life that makes you feel good.

8. **Surroundings** — Believe it or not but where you live matters. There's a power in "place." This may seem odd when talking about being an effective leader, but it has its influences. Finding out your position and thoughts in this arena could be life changing, all the way around.

After you have answered a question or done an exercise it's important to reflect on your answer or result. Why did I give that answer? What do I want to continue? What can I do differently? What results do I want? And so on. If you do so, you can take big steps forward — with small means. I base my program on the idea that, if you can get basic control over each of these eight areas and do what's best for your mind, body and soul, you'll have the best conditions for excellent health, energy and prosperity. In fact, they will become second nature very soon.

To get the entire picture, read along as I share how I worked with my client, Eric. You can achieve the same results! His process will show you how you can. You may even see a bit of yourself in him, and the issues he's facing. If you commit to making changes, which are never a "do it and done with it" deal — it's a process — and if you focus on taking one step at a time, you can change your life. You just have to start.

Meet Eric

I met Eric the same way I meet most of my clients. He was being treated for lower back pain by a physiotherapist in a Health Care Center. During one of their sessions Eric broke down and let everything out. The physiotherapist referred him to me and we had a short "get-to-know-each-other" talk by Skype and agreed to start a program.

Here's his story.

Eric, 45, is an IT-technician who has worked for the same technology company for 15 years. For the last five, he's managed a team of 25 and in the last year, the team has moved from being almost "perfect," to failing. Upper management is concerned, the customers are complaining, and increased discord among team members has turned coffee-breaks into toxic "complaint corners."

The stress factor is skyrocketing — with no time for reflection. He's avoiding interaction with his colleagues and team, is becoming forgetful, missing critical meetings and feels like he doesn't have the energy to face the snowballing issues in front of him. To complicate matters, he's had no time for physical activity, something he used to engage in on a regular basis, and when he gets the chance to eat, its junk food and generally at the wrong time, so he's gained a lot of weight, and his muscles are painfully stiff. Because his work involves evening meetings, he has begun to drink more alcoholic beverages which compound the fact that he's not sleeping well as he lays awake for hours thinking about the problems at the office.

It's not just problems at the office now either. His irritability has made him a challenge to be around so his wife of 40 years, Karin, is

becoming increasingly distant, and he rarely sees his two children —
ages 11 and 13. Although this is definitely not what he wants, he has no
idea how to change it — how to start taking care of himself. He wants
to feel better and do a better job at work and with his family, but he feels
like the whole situation is slipping out of his hands.

At his last health check-up, the doctor noted that his blood pres-
sure was slightly raised. He had been on medication for hypertension
in the past, and diabetes runs in his family. He's overweight, fatigued,
isolated and more. By the time we meet, he feels hopeless and, quite
frankly, scared.

So we begin my program:

Dr Annika´s Work Model:

First sessions with me consist of a full day in-person workshop. During
the workshop-day we eat healthy meals to show as an example and
we do at least one "Walk & Talk" session. About a week prior to the
session, you receive an e-mail link for a personality and motivational
assessment created by Ensize. It takes about 25 minutes to complete
the questions. We set a date for our initial session, often held at my
office, where we review the assessment and set the road forward. I
advise people to move out of their usual surroundings for work like
this for three reasons: the usual distractions can't occur (e.g. people
stopping in and disrupting the flow, memories, environmental stressors, etc.); you get away from the "history sitting in the walls" which
might prevent you from seeing the whole picture about yourself — it
can be quite emotional; and finally, it's private.

Five subsequent sessions are held via Skype, each around 2 hours.
We glance at all pieces of the wheel of life every time, but dive more
deeply into the most critical pieces, depending on the individual and
where they are in the process.

The sixth and final two- to four-hour wrap-up session usually is in person at my office. We summarize key successes, and lay out a strategy for the next 12 months. Sometimes I continue to "hold hands" on the journey; sometimes the client embarks on his or her own.

Content: To identify any problems and determine where you want to go, you first have to get to know who you are and where you are. I see four pieces in this:

1. Personality type — what are your motivations, what is your communication style? This is not a deep psychological analysis, and it's not an intelligence test — it's about who you are, and how you interact with others.
2. Life Circumstance — what is your current station in life? What's your environment?
3. Lifestyle — how do you take care of yourself today, and how you plan to in the future?
4. Health — what are the hard facts about your health today — diseases, weight, height, waist measure, etc.?

When done with this you may answer the following questions:

+ What do you actually win if you change the situation and behavior?
+ What do you win staying behind in the same situation and behavior?
+ Do you really want to change it?
+ What different story would you like to tell ahead when dealing with your capability and your value?

Depending on your answers, you'll know if you really are ready for a change. You are the only person able to change your life! You picked this book for a reason, so no matter how you're feeling about a change right now — whether you're ready to go, or just testing the waters, you may benefit from the information I'm sharing. Read the chapters you find most interesting. What do you have to lose?

CHAPTER 1

Self-Development – The Man in the Mirror

"Long-lasting change that will help you create new habits and actions requires an inside-out approach, as well as two very important tools: the mirror and time."

— *Darren L. Johnson*

PERSONAL DEVELOPMENT is about getting to know yourself better — without judgment. It's not about right, wrong, good, bad, indifferent — it's about how *it is*. Learning about what motivates you, what's important to you, and why you do what you do, and say what you say, is empowering. Knowing exactly who you are, without judgment or reservation raises your self-confidence — you become at ease with yourself, and those around you, even in tough situations.

There are many ways to begin this journey. You can read books, see a life coach or psychoanalyst, attend seminars, ask your friends what they think, participate in retreats — the list is endless. I find that getting to the core of our personalities first, is the best way to start. Based on years of experience in personal development, the most effective method I've found is to begin with a comprehensive behavior style analysis (DISC) developed by Ensize, an international company based in Stockholm, Sweden. Their DISC model is called "The Puzzle" and it's used to understand and describe human behavior and communication. It's easy to do and the report generated based on individual responses provides materials for life-long learning about who you are.

The Ensize/DISC Model

The Ensize/DISC instrument provides valuable information about how people behave in their environment. According to the model, there are four different types of behavior. In "The Puzzle," analysis colors are used as a simple way to describe different communication and behavior styles. All four colors are represented, but vary in strength

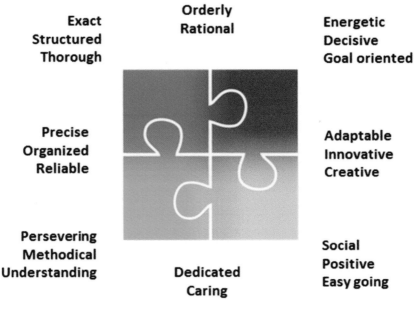

Exact
Structured
Thorough

Orderly
Rational

Energetic
Decisive
Goal oriented

Precise
Organized
Reliable

Adaptable
Innovative
Creative

Persevering
Methodical
Understanding

Dedicated
Caring

Social
Positive
Easy going

Ensize puzzle

from one style to another. Our individual communication style is a blend from all four colors. Usually one or two (and sometimes even three colors) are prominent. It's a blend of colors that gives our very own personal communication style and puts us in a specific spot on the "communication map."

Here's a short review of the properties in four colors — having much or having little. You can use it to classify yourself or to try to pinpoint your network.

Red — Dominance
A lot of red: People with a lot of red in their profile are by nature somewhat suspicious and don't always trust other people. They're often good at problem solving and take on challenges full speed ahead. They're often perceived as demanding, driving, aggressive, powerful, wayward and groundbreaking.

A little red: People with only a small amount of red are, on the other hand, retracted and timid. They want more time and information before they take a stand. They can be described as conservative, cooperative, careful, modest and peaceful.

Yellow — Influence
A lot of yellow: People with a lot of yellow in their profile tend to have a positive attitude towards the environment. They are skilled communicators and affect others by their enthusiasm and good verbal skills. They can be described as persuasive, inspiring, optimistic, sociable and trustful.

A little yellow: People with little yellow in their profile, on the other hand, often are withdrawn, reserved and controlled. They're not very communicative and prefer to affect others by data and numbers, not by feelings. They can be described as controlled, reserved, skeptical, pessimistic and critical.

Green — Stability

A lot of green: People with a lot of green in their profile like safety and friendly relations. They like to work in teams and are often persistent and methodical. They prefer to work at their own pace and to avoid changes. They can be described as calm, loyal, relaxed, patient and perserving.

A little green: People with little green in their profile, on the other hand, thrive on variety and hustle and bustle. They're open to innovations and change. They can be described as spontaneous, impatient, restless, eager and impulsive.

Blue — Conformity

A lot of blue: People with a lot of blue in their profile are aware of rules and regulations and the consequences of breaking them. They are often meticulous, quality conscious and principled people who want to do things right from the beginning. They can be described as cautious, accurate, vigilant and quality minded.

A little blue: People with little blue in their profile, on the other hand, often are independent, individualistic and fearless people. They see rules more like guidelines that you sometimes need to derogate. They can be seen as independent, rebellious, unconventional and challenging.

When we get stressed, we usually fall back on the downsides of our behavior style and react in a way we don't recognize as our natural behavior. That means that we act the opposite way from what we usually do — structured people become disorganized, calm people get impatient, etc.

To get an even better view of who you are, you can complement The Ensize Puzzle with The Ensize Carrot, which shows what makes us want to go on — what motivates us to continue doing what we're doing. It's about our deep down values and attitudes which determine our natural behavior. It helps us see clearly what we identify as right or wrong. When what we do is in synch with our values, we feel great — it's when we engage in activities that don't line up with who we are that the problems begin. The following seven driving forces are taken directly from the Ensize model:

> Individuals whose main driving force is **Knowledge** are mainly interested in discovery, fact-finding and information. "It is a pleasure to know things!" These individuals like to adopt contemplative attitudes and often ignore an object's beauty, practical use or financial value. Individuals whose driving force is knowledge want to find and understand the relationships between things. They observe reality through critical and rational eyes.

> Individuals whose main driving force is **Economic** have a strong interest in money. They focus on profitability and want to see financial returns on their investments. Investments can be in the form of both time and money. People whose driving force is financial strive to achieve the security brought by financial success. They may feel the need to outdo others when it comes to financial and material success.

> Individuals whose main driving force is **Self-fulfillment** are keenly interested in personal development and

wellbeing. People who are driven by self-fulfillment value environments which leave room for creativity and innovative thinking. The need for personal development may be expressed as a wish to put one's own or other people's ideas to the test. Internal reflection and feedback are natural working methods, which means that these individuals will appreciate environments which allow this.

Individuals whose main driving force is **Practical** appreciate careful creation and a sensible use of resources. Manufacture and creation are key concepts in this driving force. People with a practical driving force have an eye for things which may come in handy and be put to practical use. They are often good with their hands and have the capacity to start up, manage and complete projects. They like to show others what they have produced or created.

Individuals whose main driving force is **Consideration** are interested in other people, their teamwork and their wellbeing. They are often seen as friendly, pleasant and unselfish. They are occasionally willing to sacrifice their own profit (making money) if it would turn out to be a loss to someone else. People who have such a strong sense of consideration may feel that people who are driven by forces such as knowledge, practicality and leadership are indifferent and insensitive.

Individuals whose main driving forces are **Power — influence** seek control and power. The need for control can be expressed in different ways, partly as self-control and partly as control over other people. Individuals whose driving force is leadership look above all for personal power, influence and praise. With influential people it is often important to understand the ground rules and maintain a good relationship. Their driving force can also be expressed as a desire to control important decisions and decide when and how resources are to be used.

Individuals with an **Ethical — moral** driving force are characterized by a desire for justice. This can appear as a wish to work in organizations with clear structures, rules and common standards and values. The main interest behind this can be described as wanting to support the ""good forces"" behind the organization or the society as a whole.

Of the seven, pick four which you identify with the most — or seem the strongest — and these are the forces which make you, you! Combine this with your communication style, and voila! Here's your unique combination of attributes that tell you many things about who you are, how and why you do things, and, of course, how you interact with other people. This is so important because the way other people react to you, is actually based on who you are. You also begin to understand why others do things differently from you, which fosters better communication and less judgment. The more time you spend familiarizing yourself with these very different attributes, the more easily you will begin to recognize different (or similar) attributes in others, which ultimately results in less interpersonal conflict. These exercises, by the way, also are very effective in group or team development.

☐ ERIC UPDATE

At the workshop: The program begins with the Ensize behavior style analysis. Eric had filled in the questionnaire ahead of time, and I had the results. He turned out to be high in Red combined with high Blue and high Yellow in "The Puzzle," having 3 dominant colors. In his adapted behavior he tuned in on more red. His primary driving force in "The Carrot" was "Practical" and the second, "Knowledge."

Eric has always seen himself as a good man — he's social, nice to everybody, does a good job, has things in order, easily generates new contacts, both business and personal, etc. In fact, he believes these qualities got him the leadership position in his company.

When we start talking about this, Eric suddenly says he's lost all that — he has no self-confidence and the job is not fun anymore. Life is not fun. He is worthless. He says he's felt this way for a long time, but it's the first time he's said it aloud and he feels relieved. These feelings have scared him so much and he has not felt it possible to reveal "the truth" to anyone, not even his wife. Here's where progress begins. What is the truth, really? Who is that man in the mirror?

A person with Eric's communication style (high Red with high Blue and Yellow) and his strong motivators (practical-knowledge) is a person who knows his thing. He's methodical (anything random makes him uncomfortable) and uses his resources in a practical and economical way. He also is very hands-on, relies on earlier experiences, and can usually do the job very well himself.

When Eric sees this he gets a big smile on his face and says: "You're talking about me! Well, the 'me' that I was, before things got out of hand." As we continue reviewing his Ensize results, he's smiling and nodding his head constantly. "This is all about me, he says, and what a great goldmine to dig from. I'd almost forgotten who I am! Now I recognize the man in the mirror." We continue by defining the colors and what they mean, how things are connected and how you can see what "color" other people are, and how you can use that knowledge in a team. Eric is very excited about sharing this with his team — a workshop format where they all do the analysis and then use a variety of tools to get to know each other better.

☐ End of Month 1

He's been busy addressing other areas so has not specifically addressed this one. He revisits the results now and then, to boost his self-confidence, but has taken no action.

☐ End of Month 2

He's been primarily focused on other issues requiring substantive time, so he's not done anything specifically in this area. He had asked his closest team members to ask for the interest about doing a workshop with the group. They were to report before next feedback session.

☐ End of Month 3

There seemed to be interest from the group, so they included a workshop in future plans.

☐ End of Month 4

He's feeling better now, and the team has set a date for the workshop.

☐ End of Month 5

Workshop planned in 2 weeks. He has assigned to one team-member to do the practical arrangements. I've sent the links to all of the materials so they will have the report ready prior to the workshop.

☐ End of Month 6

He feels he has control over, and is a comrade among his group again for the first time in a long time. He has continually reflected on his analysis and is regaining personal control, thereby working better with his group. In fact, the workshop was outstanding. According to Eric, "they laughed together like they had never before. Even the guys who had been most negative had thawed up and were participating." He could see joy was back in the group — even more than before. They had also developed a "common language" through the colors, which helped them communicate openly and honestly, without feeling offended.

CHAPTER **2**

Health:
You Can't Live Without It

"The first wealth is health."

— Ralph Waldo Emerson

S O HOW DO YOU CARE for yourself? How do you care for your body? Do you exercise? How do you eat? Do you sleep well? How do you manage stress? Do you use stimulants like caffeine or over the counter "pick-me-ups" or other substances that help "shift" your mood or energy levels?

All of these issues play a key role in optimum health. We've come a long way in our understanding of good health and all that it entails — it's the basis for everything and it's extremely complex. The most important thing we do know is that lifestyle factors affect or create health issues such as cardiovascular disease, diabetes, obesity, cancer, inflammatory diseases, and depression, among many others. I would say that more than 75% of the patients I see at the Health Care Center come with issues that could have been avoided by a healthier life style. The good news here is this: our choices today can change outcomes for tomorrow. There's always great potential for improvement.

In this chapter we will go through some key areas that impact health, but as you will see, they are all connected. If you make improvements in one area, it will spill over to the next. Please note that if you are dealing with a serious illness, I would advise you work with your doctor to choose one area to address. Although one action will not cure your disease, it may reduce the risk of progression or additional illness. It's never too late to start taking care of your body and mind.

Sleep

Why do we spend time sleeping? Seems like a big waste of time, doesn't it? If we use those hours for work we will get so much more done — right?

Wrong. Human beings need sleep. Though the amount necessary varies by individual, everyone needs quality sleep to survive. What's this all about? Seems we know a lot about what happens during sleep, and what happens when we don't sleep, but we don't know as much about *why* we need sleep.

We need to get back to basic biology to understand. If we understand how sleep is meant to work then it is much easier to understand what happens when it doesn't work properly.

Current research divides sleep into 5 stages.

Stage 1: Falling asleep

Brief time — 5–10 minutes. Easily aroused. Heart rate and blood pressure on its way down. Easiest to fall asleep is if we follow the body's day clock and go to bed when melatonin, the sleep hormone, is starting to be excreted — for most people this occurs in the hours before midnight.

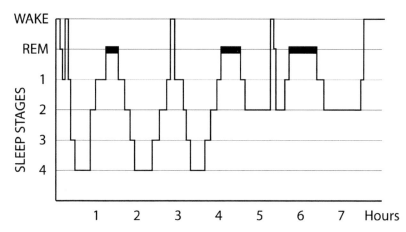

Sleep Stages

Stage 2: Normal sleeping

Still fairly easily aroused by normal speaking in the same room. Sometimes called "empty sleep," it covers about half the time of sleep during the night. Body temperature decreases, breathing gets slower and the heart rate slows down.

Stage 3 and 4: Deep sleep

Stage 3 is just for a short time before entering the most soothing sleep — stadium 4. At this stage we are difficult to wake and will usually only be woken by a stimulus important to the individual — like a mother wakening by her baby's cry. Heart rate and breathing rate drop further, as does blood pressure. Most of the growth hormone is released during this time and most of the central nervous systems recovery is been done here. Most of the stage 3–4 that we need are during the first 3½ hours of sleep.

Dream sleep — also called REM (rapid eye movement)

This is the stage in which we dream and our eyes flicker. Sleep is shallow and we are more easily aroused. Breathing, heart rate and

13

blood pressure raises but muscle tonus is still low — our big muscle groups get temporarily de-attached and we are temporarily lame to ensure we don't get up and start acting out the dream. Body temperature is also shut off during this stage. We usually have longer periods of this in the second half of nighttime.

A healthy adult usually requires anywhere from six to nine hours of sleep each night. Women need a little more sleep than men and they often have more sleeping problems. The latest very interesting research, from the Surrey University in Great Britain, shows that during sleep more than 1800 genes are affected, many of them regulating our basal metabolism. When sleeping less than 6 hours per night for a week at least 400 of these genes are greatly disturbed in a negative way in their normal function affecting the possibility of diseases like diabetes, obesity, cardiovascular, stress and aging. These interesting results show us how essential sleep is to a good and healthy life. So sleeping is really not a waste of time, it is a source for life.

As we grow older, though, our need for sleep decreases. A normal 60-year-old requires only six hours of sleep. The reason for this, most scientists agree, is that during the "dream sleep" stage, we process things going on around us. As we grow older, we process things differently so we don't need as much "dream sleep."

Sleep is essential for a healthy life. During sleep the body repairs or disposes of damaged cells, and the brain is refreshed. While we sleep, our body takes inventory and does its housecleaning, so to speak. Occasional nights without sleep usually are not harmful to your health. The body takes care of itself and people usually have a deeper sleep the following night.

Disturbed sleep is often a first sign when your body and mind have had too much. And we all know that lack of sleep can cause you to become irritable and distracted. You can do with one or two nights without sleep, but if you miss more than that on a regular basis, there can be serious consequences: your job performance may suffer; the risk for accidents, both at home and on the road, will increase; your immune system will be compromised; your metabolism may change; and your risk for obesity and cardiovascular disease substantially increases.

Yes, a couple of drinks, or sleeping pills make you sleepy initially. But the sleep you actually get as a result is not physiologically beneficial. Well sleeping pill *may* be a solution for a short time if your need for sleep is bad.

Feeling good about yourself is the best sleeping pill of all. This goes well in hand with working with yourself, getting to know yourself better and taking control of your situation. One tool to use is to think about three things to be thankful for that happened during the day. It doesn't have to be big things, maybe just someone giving you a smile, a good meal you had or something you finished in your work. Be generous and kind to yourself.

Sleep must be seen as one of the most essential thing to change first. All the issues are connected but sleep is so central to everything, it should be a top priority. If you do have trouble sleeping, here are some recommendations to help you create conditions that encourage sleep.

By end of the day, it's important to wind down the pace of life. End you day with a short evening walk or with a hot bath. Regular physical activity not closer than 2–3 hours before bedtime. Engaging in a relatively quiet activity so the brain can tune down and prepare for sleep. Don't eat big meals close to bedtime, but don't go to bed hungry either. Turn down the light and, if possible, do a short meditation before falling asleep.

Make your room a place for sleep. Make it cooler (16–18 C) and quiet. Turn off any machines in the room, you might not hear them at daytime with all background noise but when it gets quiet even a subdued sound can be very annoying and prevent you from relaxing enough to fall asleep. Keep it clean; remove clutter or anything that might disturb your thoughts. The bedroom is for sleep, not work.

Check your bed, pillow, blanket and sheets. Clean and soft, cotton, ironed bed sheets are ideal — they actually send positive signals to our brain through the feeling in the skin. Size of bed ideal if + 40 cm on the width and + 20 cm of length compared to your body.

I'll bet you can guess what I'm going to suggest you do next — that's right! A **Sleep Diary**. For one week, take a good look at your current sleeping situation. It will reveal what you need to change and make it possible to start getting healthy, restorative sleep. (For a sample, and downloadable form, see Appendix A.)

☐ ERIC UPDATE

At the workshop: When we first met, Eric couldn't remember the last time he'd a good night's sleep. And he used to be a sound sleeper. When he first became a manager, he was happy, peaceful, and everything went well. Soon, however, his head started to "spin" with thoughts about the workday, issues he needed to resolve, goals that weren't being met, etc. and he began to have difficulty falling asleep. He had many business events and dinners to attend — often with too much wine or beer — which did make him relax, but he still felt tired the next morning. It wasn't bad at first, but after about a year he felt exhausted — all day, every day — so he began to make mistakes he would not have made if he were well rested and his mind were clear.

He and Karin share bedroom. Her part of the room is nice and tidy, she just has a clock and a book on her bed table. His side of the room? Stacks of paper, dirty clothes, and many other things he hasn't had time to go through and sort out. Karin doesn't want to sort his stuff so, over time, his side looks like a war zone.

Eric was in for some hard work.

Task #1: Prepare the sleep diary to take home and do for two weeks.

Task #2: Organize the mess; send pictures of before and after.

☐ End of Month 1

Update Task #1: Eric sent his sleep diary to me. It demonstrated a distinct correlation to bad sleep when he'd been drinking alcohol on weeknights. It also showed his sleeping hours were not only irregular, but disrupted, as he woke up in the middle of every night to urinate.

Update Task #2: He did tidy up his bedroom, and agreed to keep it that way through our mentoring time.

New Task #3: Reduce alcohol on weeknights. He was not prepared to stop drinking all together but we agreed on him having "every second glass" of water instead. Because of his need to get up in the middle of the night every night, he also was to be aware of not drinking too much (of anything) right before going to bed.

New Task #4: Establish a regular bed time. His goal was to be in bed before midnight every night.

☐ End of Month 2

Update Task #2: Bedroom still tidy — though he used to "drop" things just anywhere, he realizes it's much nicer now.

Update Task #3: He's very proud to announce he's been drinking more water than beer or wine.

Update Task #4: Only once, after a birthday dinner party, has he missed his midnight bedtime.

His stomach ache is almost gone and he feels generally more energized.

New Task #5: Now that he's feeling better and things are tidier, he's noticed his bed is very old and shabby. Next month he will look for a new bed.

New Task #6: He still has problems with nightly toilet visits and he is referred to his family doctor to have his prostate examined.

☐ **End of Month 3**

Still keeping up his good work with less alcohol, regular sleep hours, and regulated liquid intake. Has not had time to look for new bed.

☐ **End of Month 4**

Update Task #5: After realizing their beds were 20 years old, Eric and Karin bought new beds, pillows and blankets.

Update Task #6: His visit to the doctor proved highly beneficial, as he was diagnosed with a benign large prostate and began treatment.

☐ **End of Month 5**

> The prostate medication worked so he now sleeps all night and is feeling better than he has in a long time.

☐ **End of Month 6**

> At our in-person wrap-up — a mere 6 months later — Eric is a happy, well-sleeping man. Keeping the bedroom tidy is now a piece of cake. He feels joy every night going to bed in his soft nice sheets in a nice comfy bed. His alcohol consumption is minimal, and he has far fewer nights out due to work obligations.

Diet — Nourishment and Food Choices

There are so many different opinions about what to eat, when to eat, how to eat and countless variations of diets, weight reduction programs, vitamin supplements and so on. Many are expensive and don't provide the nutrients, energy or comfort your body receives from eating real food.

To complicate the issue, food not only is required for nourishment, but accompanying our food choices are deep-seated feelings and memories. We use food for all types of celebrations, but we also can use or abuse it to numb feelings, or escape — almost like a drug. Obesity currently is a global epidemic (the World Health Organization refers to it as "globesity"), and unfortunately, diseases like diabetes, arthritis, high blood pressure and coronary heart disease are an inevitable result.

There's no need to go overboard and create crazy deprived "food rules" for yourself, but you do need to try to think about it differently. Grandma's cookies may say "I love you," but have two or three, not ten or twenty. If you think of food as way to nourish your body giving you energy to participate in your life, rather than stimulate (or placate) your emotions, you will find you can make a dramatic shift in your food choices in a relatively short period of time. To make the best of our need for nourishment, I have three rules: consistency, consistency, and consistency. I also have a short, easy rule to remember about food: 3-2-1. Eat **3 main meals** and **2** (or 3) **small snacks** during the day to balance your blood sugar, keep your energy levels up, and keep your cravings for sweets or junk food to a minimum, and eat just **1 serving** each meal. Choose to eat a little bit of everything.

The normal rule is to try to get 10% of your energy from fats, 50–60% from carbs and 10–20% of the energy from proteins. However this isn't a very practical way to think every time you eat, and it's pretty complicated. For this reason, I'd like to give you some examples of how to think about the kinds of nutrients and the amounts rather than telling you exactly what to eat.

Here's the breakdown you should aim for — once you understand the basic approach of food combinations for optimum nourishment, you can be as creative as you'd like.

Meal and Calorie Breakdown

(One serving per meal on a standard plate — diameter 24 cm)

Breakfast ¼ of calories of the day
(You've heard it a million times, and that's because it's true — breakfast is the most important meal of the day. It jumpstarts your metabolic system, and your brain, and keeps you on the right track throughout the day so make it count.)

Lunch ⅓ of calories of day

Dinner: ¼ of calories of day (like lunch but slightly smaller portion)

Snacks: ⅕ of calories of day

The plate model is a tool to get the right proportions between the different foods you need. The plate model is dividing the plate in three parts. The proportions of the parts depend on what you aim for — see below. This makes it easy to remember when you make your serving:

Part One: Carbohydrates — potatoes, pasta, rice, couscous, bulgur, noodles and such. Bread also belongs here. (2–3 medium size potatoes/2–3 dl cooked rise/equivalent and maybe 1 slice of bread with 5–10 grams of butter per serving)

Part Two: Fruits and Vegetables — vegetables, roots and fruits that contain important vitamins, minerals, antioxidants and fibers. All in all around 500 grams per day, equals for example 3 fruits and 2 big scoops of vegetables.

Basic Plate Model

Part Three: Protein — meat, fish, eggs or a vegetarian alternative like lenses, chickpeas or beans. They give us both proteins and important minerals like iron, zinc and selenium. All in all around 200–250 grams pure meat/fish or equivalents per day (125–150 grams for lunch and 100–125 grams for supper)

The plate model can be adjusted for different needs. The principle and platesize is the same for all different needs but you adjust the proportions based on your particular needs.

When **you need less energy** (e.g. you sit still a lot, or you want to lose weight) make part 2 (greens and roots) half the plate and reduce part 1 with the same amount. Part 3 is always the same.

When you **need more energy** (e.g. you work hard or engage in a lot of physical activity) do the reverse. Part 1 (carbs) is made half the plate and part 2 is reduced the same amount. Again, part three remains the same.

When dining out it's not always easy to pick and choose, but many restaurants will work with you if you ask them. And it's ok if you're not perfect every day, as long as you do right most days. One way to pay attention to what you're eating on a daily basis is a **Diet Diary**. Write everything, *yes everything*, you put in your mouth down for at least two weeks. When done, take a good look at it. Were you honest to yourself and added everything? Next look at the total — does it fit with the plate model thinking? What improvements can you make? Write them down. (For a sample, and downloadable form, see Appendix B.)

The fundamental truth about your body's weight is that it's primarily about the following: calories — calories in and calories out; what you eat; when you eat; and how you eat. One easy thing you can do for your diet and your health, without committing to any difficult formulas, is to eat more fruits and vegetables — ideally 500 grams per day. They supply your body with the antioxidants necessary to mend broken cells and improve your immune system. The different colors of fruits and vegetables represent specific antioxidants, so eat a variety — 3 colors a day is optimum. Fruits and vegetables are also a good source of fiber that will enhance the function of your digestive system.

A final note about consumption. Think about this — say you attend a dinner party — drinks, a 3 course meal (all of which include wine) and then a small night meal. This one meal makes up more calories than you need for the entire day (in some cases more)! Don't get me wrong, you may treat yourself regularly — but always in moderation.

☐ ERIC UPDATE

At the workshop: Food currently is a disaster in Eric's life. It wasn't always like this, but since he was promoted, healthy eating fell to the way side due to a number of factors — he felt he was too busy to eat regularly scheduled, healthy meals, and he was required to attend frequent evening dinner meetings so his alcohol consumption increased dramatically. He gained weight rather quickly, and it didn't take long before his entire system started to go haywire — heartburn, acid reflux, digestive issues, and more. Needless to say, his physical state made his mood terrible as well.

During our initial "get to know yourself" session, we established Eric's current health:

Height: 185 cm

Weight: 97 kg

Body Mass Index (BMI): 29 (Eric is overweight: <25 is normal; 25–30 is overweight; and >30 is obese)

Waist Measurement: 110 cm (indicating a highly increased risk for cardiovascular complications)

For men — minimal risk for cardiovascular complications < 94 cm, increased risk 94–102 cm, highly increased risk for cardio-vascular complications > 102 cm;

For Women — minimal risk 80 cm, increased risk 80–88 cm, highly increased risk for cardiovascular complications >88 cm). Today science indicates that waist measurements are much better correlated to cardiovascular disease than BMI.

Task #1: Do the Diet Diary for two weeks.

☐ End of Month 1

Update Task #1: Eric was not happy with this exercise initially, but he obliged and documented his eating patterns for the two weeks following our workshop day. He actually continued until our next call. During the workshop we had talked a lot about his lousy diet habits and during that day he did get food according to the good rules. The exercise made him feel so guilty it literally made him sick. But he did his homework and during his follow up session, we discussed it again. It was nice to see that during the month he kept track he slowly changed his eating patterns. He was not aware of it until we talked about it, but he had noticed his stomach was feeling much better and his heartburn was gone — although he did admit he'd gotten a two week treatment of Omeprazol to help with the acid reflux.

New Task #2: Get his breakfasts in order.

☐ End of Month 2

Update Task #2: Breakfast is now in order. He feels better during the mornings and keeps his energy up until by lunch by eating a piece of fruit at 10:00 a.m. He's extended the good morning feeling to the entire department by having a fruit delivered daily to his department.

New Task #3: Lunch still needs a little work. Together we've created ideas based on the plate model.

☐ End of Month 3

Update Task #3: Lunch is now in order, although it's been a little trickier than breakfast at home. He and his team have checked out nearby restaurants and rated them — some are ok others are not. He's perused the grocery store easy-to-make or frozen meals, and has found a few that he feels are ok, especially if you complete them with some fresh vegetables. And, he's started a trend in the office: leftover from home. It turns out there was some embarrassment initially, among the entire team, about bringing leftover — but by setting a good example, they now have begun discussing good and bad eating habits.

New Task #4: He's getting there — but evening meals still need a little work. Again, together we've created ideas based on the plate model.

☐ End of Month 4

Update Task #4: Evening meals are no problem when eating at home. He and Karin have started to cook together and engage the children as well. He has still not solved the eating out with clients issue — but he does have the alcohol part under control.

Until next month he just keeps the good work up that he has done so far.

☐ **End of Month 5**

It is so easy to get into the "so little time so I'll just quickly grab junk food" trap when you're hungry. But he's aware of the problem now, and that makes it a little bit easier on him.

New Task #5: Document how many times he's eaten out for the last year and present that at our 6-month meeting.

☐ **End of Month 6**

Update Task #5: Eric had at least 1 evening out each week up until 6 months ago. After that it slowly decreased and last month — it was only once. He now realizes the incremental changes he's been making are adding up — he's changed quite a bit! Although he admits food is hard for him — it's easy to get off track — he's much more aware, and less judgmental of himself when he's not perfect.

The next assignment? Complete the diet diary — we'll compare it to the one he completed six months ago and he'll be surprised at how well he's doing now, with seemingly little effort.

Physical Activity

The human body is made to move. You've heard the saying use it or lose it? This is the hard fact about our bodies — we're designed for movement. Inactivity not only causes your muscles to become stiff and achy, but scientific studies have shown that sitting still is even more hazardous to your health than smoking, and can increase the risk of cardiovascular disease. And the benefits of being active don't stop at the body. Physical activity does the following: enhances the mind, promoting clear and vivid thinking, as well as better problem-solving capabilities, eliminates stress hormones *and* it impacts weight, blood pressure, blood sugar, cholesterol levels and so much more.

Much of this information is not new — at the most basic level, exercise strengthens the heart muscles which in turn enhances lung function making the circulatory system work more efficiently, and keeping our muscles from atrophy. Though most studies to date indicated a brisk 30 minute walk each day, in addition to 2–3 strength building workouts per week, was enough, new research is showing it's not enough to engage in "bursts" of physical activity, a few times a week — we must be active on a more continuous basis.

I personally believe that both things count. We need to reduce our "sitting still" time and have bursts of physical activity. If your work involves sitting at a desk all day long, take mini-breaks frequently to stretch and move around a little — at least twice an hour. And it's never too late to start a fitness program. Just be sure you know what your body is ready for and train accordingly to prevent injury.

So, start moving! Your body will become leaner; you will have more energy, feel less pain — you will even think more clearly!

And guess what I suggest to help you get started — a **Physical Activity Diary**. I know I'm having you write a lot of information down, but it works. Most people are not aware of their daily habits which impact their overall health, so when beginning the process of change, it's helpful to really see where you're at, what you're currently doing and what needs to change.

If you record your activities for one week, you will have a good idea of how truly active you are. (For a sample, and downloadable form, see Appendix C.)

Moving the body will recharge your energy level, your anxiety will decrease and your thinking will become clear again. Try moving around — even if it's just a short walk down the hall — the next time stress gets to you and you'll find yourself feeling much more relaxed and at ease.

For some, the thought of moving almost continuously seems unachievable — but here's the deal: it all counts! Consider incorporating the following into your daily routine:

- Take "Walk & Talk" coffee breaks, instead of sitting in the lunch room
- Park the car in the far corner of the parking lot
- Get off the bus one station early and walk the rest
- Use the stairs instead of the elevator or escalator
- Put your printer in another room, or down the hallway
- Get up and use the on/off button on the TV instead of the remote control
- At home — cleaning/laundry/gardening

Complement these everyday movements with daily power walks and going to the gym (or equivalent) 2–3 times a week and you will achieve a good basic level of physical activity. Use every chance you have to make a move — don't sit still for long!

It's important to address another current physical issue facing us all here — the overuse of specific muscle groups engaging in repetitive movement (e.g. tennis elbow, mouse arm, among others.) As soon as you notice pain from such repetitive activity you are best helped if you stop doing it and try to relax those areas. Here are some tips that will help prevent some damage while SMSing, sitting at your computer, etc.:

- Take regular breaks
- Look straight ahead every 5 minutes. Draw your lower jaw toward the neck, and keep that position for a few seconds.
- Rotate your shoulders while keeping your arms alongside your body (this will increase blood flow to the shoulders.)
- Sit up straight
- Hold any device (mobile phone, ipad, etc.) up higher when in use

☐ ERIC UPDATE

At the workshop: Eric was an athlete as a young man — a soccer champ! As the years passed, however, he lost interest and like many he found a new love — technology. As time passed, he became much less active. Although he did run regularly, and went to a gym twice a week, he began to decrease these activities as his work responsibilities increased. And so began a vicious cycle — he gained weight, which made exercise not as enjoyable — even difficult — so he gained more weight, etc. He had no interest at this point in diving into to a physical activity program. So, we started with the "Daily natural physical activity" list, see above.

Task #1: Physical Activity Diary: Write down every single thing you do during the day that can be counted as an activity — include what it is, how long it took, and how difficult it was. Do this for two weeks.

Task #2: Record three favorite activities and list pros and cons of engaging. (Name anything — ballgames, team sports, jogging, biking, etc.)

☐ End of Month 1

Update Task #1: Together, we reviewed his Physical Activity Diary. He didn't log many hours sitting completely still, which was good, but he didn't raise his rate in any way — or engage in any physical activity that made him sweat, or at least be warm.

Update Task #2: He'd indicated his love for jogging earlier, but his weight brought complications to this type of exercise at this point. We agreed that as he'd done with the other activities, we'd set a goal and move toward it in small increments. Start by walking and by the end of six months — run a 5km loop. Until next call he was to walk as fast as he could.

☐ End of Month 2

Update Task #2: He's now walking his 5 km loop comfortably in 45 minutes. His current goal is to walk 3 times a week but it usually ends at two. He's also begun to use his walk time to solve work issues. He takes one issue each walk, and carries pen and paper along to jot down ideas that come to him that he can use. He's realizing the impact the time is having on his thinking and is feeling much more energized.

☐ End of Month 3

Update Task #2: He's now jogging the 5 Km loop in 30 minutes and he tries to do it 3 or 4 times a week, but not every week. His energy levels continue to increase, while his waist is decreasing — he's very proud.

☐ End of Month 4

Update Task #2: Still jogging in 30 minutes, mostly 4 times a week. He keeps writing his activity diary.

New Task #3: He will now also start to implement something like this at work. He's advised the team to use Walk & Talk meetings when they need to discuss things.

☐ End of Month 5

Update Task #2: He's started to run short bits of the loop and is feeling great!

Update Task #3: With increasing dissention among the ranks about the Walk & Talk meetings (they find it more time consuming), we discuss the fact that although it might seem to take a little longer initially, in the long run they make better decisions, with fewer faults and they actually feel better. In other words, if they commit to the time upfront, it proves much more efficient in the long run.

☐ End of Month 6

A mere six months later, Eric was again a fit man. He had lost 33 lbs (15 kg) and had turned a lot of fat into muscles. His waist was down to 41 inches (104 cm), his breathing was easier and his eyes were clear and smiling. Life was so much easier. His next goal: weight lifting at the gym to continue to build muscle tone.

Update Task #3: The team has started to use Walk & Talk meetings much more frequently, finding them very effective. Inspired by Eric's progress, they've decided on a workshop to implement many more of the tools Eric has learned.

Stress

Stress is a normal condition in life and it plays dual roles in our lives. It's a result of both internal and external influences. A little bit of stress keeps us motivated and alert — "on our toes," so to speak. Prolonged or heightened stress, on the other hand, can ignite a chain of physiological events that impact both the mind and the body. We're all familiar with the "fight or flight response" — the body's automatic response that prepares to "fight" or "flee" from perceived attack, or threat to survival. When this happens, our bodies literally undergo a physical change and chemicals like adrenaline, noradrenaline and cortisol are released into our bloodstream — our heart rate increases, blood pumps into our limbs, our pupils dilate, our awareness intensifies, and more. In other words, we become prepared—physically and psychologically—for fight or flight.

Unfortunately, today it's neither accepted, or appropriate to literally fight with your perceived "enemy" — the person or situation causing you to feel stress — or to run away from the problem. When confronted with a difficult situation, we must "deal with it" — be it an angry boss, rush hour traffic, a speeding ticket, tense situation with a colleague, having too much work and not enough time, trying to process the constant barrage of information we receive on a daily basis, and so much more. This wreaks havoc on our bodies and minds — we're in a constant state of vigilance, ready for anything.

Having a few situations with this type of stress won't kill you — but prolonged stress can cause serious health complications Think about this. If the stress you are carrying was a stone — would it be light, or heavy? (Actually, the absolute weight doesn't matter.) What does matter, though, is how long you hold onto it. In an hour, your arm will ache, in a day it will feel numb, or even paralyzed. So the longer you carry it, the heavier it becomes, and the more damage is done. In each case, the weight of the stone doesn't change, but the longer you hold it, the heavier it becomes. The stresses and worries in life are like that stone. Think about them for a while and

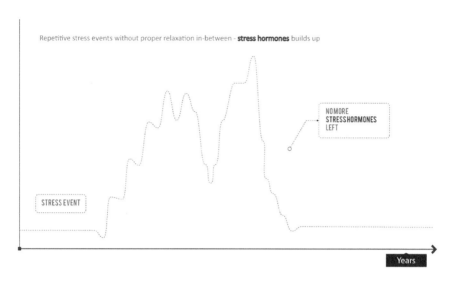

Stress Graph

nothing happens. Think about them a bit longer and they begin to hurt. And if you think about them all day long, you will feel paralyzed — incapable.

Cortisol is a hormone produced by the adrenal glands, which are located on top of the kidneys. Called the "stress hormone," it influences changes in the body in response to stress including blood sugar levels; fat, protein and carbohydrate metabolism; immune responses; blood pressure and the central nervous system. With prolonged high levels of this hormone — your blood sugar levels will elevate, which could lead to diabetes; your immune system becomes suppressed leading to more infections; and it can impact your bone structure which could lead to osteoporosis.

As you can see, if we begin to feel like we are moving from crisis to crisis, with no relief in sight, burnout is inevitable. Although the burnout is negative, it often provides motivation for serious life changes — positive life changes. It forces us to look at how things really are in our lives, and keep what's working, and toss, or deal with, the rest. Keeping a **Stress Journal** is a good way to get a picture of the real situation — write down your major stressors, which are constant, and write about situations that have caused stress. Then let it all go. (For a sample, and downloadable form, see Appendix D.)

If that doesn't work, here's simple exercise. Any time you feel out of control, or that you just can't do it, or [name the stressful situation] — take a deep breath. Slow down. Take several deep breaths, in fact. Just focus on breathing — it will bring you to the present — the here and now — and it will give you a moment away from the problem. If you need to leave the room for a minute, excuse yourself, and breathe deeply. This will give you some time to let the problem settle a little in your mind before you simply react — it will make the issue seem less "dangerous," and it actually oxygenates your brain, helping you think more clearly and avoid a potential panic attack. Don't forget to close your door when you need to — turn off the phone, give yourself a chance to focus, get up and move around for a few minutes . . . there are many ways to clear your mind so you can continue your work.

☐ ERIC UPDATE

At the workshop: Stress is a normal life condition, and Eric was a pretty easygoing man before — in fact I would say before we met, he had a relatively healthy relation to stress. He knew life could be tough sometimes; he'd had his disasters, and had tackled them well. I guess that's why people around him didn't see the warning signals he sent out, really quite soon after he was promoted to manager. It wasn't that he couldn't handle the situations one by one; he simply was ill-prepared for the increasing amount of work required, and the new relationship as manager, with his former colleagues.

The first two years he seemed fine, at least on the surface. His department had a good reputation and for some time he rested on his laurels. But as time went on, he became lonely and he really felt isolated! He felt ashamed of not being able to handle the situation when it came up, and as complaints from everywhere increased, he started to sink deeper and deeper into depression. So he drank more and more alcohol — it's a great tranquilizer, to a certain point.

When he came to the workshop his department had known for a week that he was getting help. Some had come and wished him luck but most of them said nothing.

Task #1: At the workshop we discussed his situation in its entirety and decided he would work on a stress diary for the coming few weeks to help clearly identify any weak spots and where he needed the most help.

Task #2: Breathing. When we're feeling stressed, we often hold our breath. One of the most effective ways to calm down is to simply breathe, and breathe deeply. It must be the first thought, every time we begin to feel stressed — just breathe. We practice a few times — it's all about practice. (He's also got Dr Annika's short Four Season meditation audios since meditation is a tremendous aid to stress relief.)

☐ **End of Month 1**

> **Update Task #1:** Initially, his stress diary stressed him out even more — so he stopped. He had so many other things to deal with that he had focused on those.

Update Task #2: He continued the deep breathing practice, and the meditation, and was finding it extremely helpful.

☐ End of Month 2

He's still on edge and feeling completely stressed about everything.

Update Task #2: He's making progress with deep breathing so he hasn't been feeling as panicked.

☐ End of Month 3

Update Task #2: Deep breathing begins to feels very natural.

☐ End of Month 4

Continues progress.

☐ End of Month 5

Update Task #1: He's now completed the stress diary which is helping him identify his triggers. He clearly is most stressed in the afternoon and evenings. He begins each day pretty stress-free, but by the time noon hits, and he realizes he will not be able to complete what he needs to complete, his stress levels skyrocket, making him completely ineffective. And, he does not find "to do" lists effective so he is not willing to implement this tool.

New Task #3: He does understand he needs some sort of structure to work from so he doesn't work himself into a stressed-out frenzy, so I share the **"Important/Urgent or not"** tool. (For a sample, and downloadable form, see Appendix E.)

As you can see, this tool helps categorize and prioritize activities. If Not Important/Not Urgent, it can wait. Or it could be delegated to someone else on his team. This exercise also helped Eric learn when to ask for help.

- ☐ **End of Month 6**

    Update Task #3: The "Important/Urgent or Not" tool over the last month has been a success! It's helped him prioritize, delegate, thereby becoming much more efficient, and less stressed. (Not to say that he didn't struggle with the delegation element at first.)

Substance Use

Aaah, the pleasure centers. We all have a built in craving for fun, elevated moods — good drink, good food, sugar, gambling, shopping, great sex — pleasure in general. And our brains reward this. When we are engaged in pleasurable activities, dopamine is released, and we feel happy, sometimes even euphoric. It gives us a break from the daily routine, or stressors, and makes us feel good — at least for a brief period of time.

That's all fine and good, so it seems. But using any substance to elevate our mood, or engaging in a behavior that proves to have negative long term consequences, can be dangerous — you can play with it for a while, but it won't play with you for long. It's serious business.

Addiction is a chronic disease. It is an acquired, chronic change of the brain's reward system, and the changes are the same whether it's an addiction to a substance, or a behavior. Although there's a huge amount of research on the disease, there currently are no permanent, effect methods to reverse the band once an addiction is manifested. That's why we say things like "sober alcoholic" or "gamble-free gambler." We do know there are strong inherited risk factors (but nothing you can measure), and we have shifted the definition of it being a lifestyle choice, to being a disease as serious, and difficult to treat, as cancer. The good news here is that, by releasing some of the stigma associated with addictions, people can release some of the guilt they carry and seek help and support.

Here are some things to look at if you think you might be dealing with an addiction:

- ◆ I have started to sneak around to use this substance/or engage in this behavior
- ◆ I find myself thinking about the next time I will use this substance/engage in this behavior
- ◆ I feel a craving for this substance/behavior
- ◆ I have developed a tolerance and need stronger/higher doses of this substance
- ◆ I get a "high" feeling from this substance/behavior
- ◆ I have withdrawal or negative symptoms when not using this substance/engaged in this behavior
- ◆ It affects the rest of my life, family, work
- ◆ Even after long pauses I can fall into it again

If any of these statements resonate with you, it might be time to get help.

Addiction is a complex disease, and there are varied theories on its origin, causes, effects, and treatments. The common thread, among all theories, however, is that a person is using/abusing a substance, or engaging in a behavior, that is negatively impacting the quality of their life. Although there is initial satisfaction in imbibing, or engaging, the after effect always produces guilt, and remorse. People today are addicted to numerous things — food, work, gambling, etc. For the purposes of our work, though, let's take a brief look at two of the top health issues — alcohol abuse, and cigarettes.

Alcohol is a socially accepted "drug," included in a variety of activities around the world — celebrations, business functions, social gatherings, funerals, etc. Most people drink either to feel relaxed or happy and small amounts do provide that effect. When you start to increase consumption, however, people can become agitated, angry, and may lose their ability to make sound decisions or come to rational conclusions. Excessive amounts of alcohol can lead to loss of muscle control, "passing out," and in extreme cases — death.

The problem with identifying alcohol addiction is that although a person can consume large quantities of alcohol, it's not obvious in their behavior at large. But think about this: a person addicted to alcohol, still highly functioning, can show blood levels of alcohol that would mean death to a nondrinker. It's not because they have a better way to get rid of the alcohol; it is just that their brain has gotten used to constantly be swimming in alcohol. They may seem to be "functioning" on the surface, but in truth, their thinking is muddled, and their motor skills are not functioning at their best. Alcoholism currently is a medical diagnosis. It's a progressive disease that can take years to uncover and address. Some people can stop on their own, or modify their behavior, but others need some help. There are medications that actually block the "euphoria" and cravings — thus taking away the "reward," and making it easier to not drink.

If you smoke, do you remember the first time? You probably coughed a lot. That's because your body reacted as it's supposed to — like it was being attacked by a poison and had no defense. After just the next few cigarettes, your body has created a defense by making nicotine receptors in the brain — which created a positive feeling. The more you smoke, the more receptors develops. After just a short period of time, the brain remembers the "kick" you got from the nicotine and it wants more — thus an addiction is born. The bad news about smoking it that it's highly addictive and is harmful to every single cell in the body. As many as 40 diseases are common among smokers, and their life-span is normally about 7–8 years shorter than a non-smoker. The good news is, there a many ways to quit so you can pick what works best for you. The one common denominator among people who have quit successfully is this: they were committed to quitting — they had decided to stop for good.

It's interesting to note that alcohol and smoking are intimately connected. In fact, Ninety percent of all alcoholics are addicted to nicotine as well. If you don't think you have an addiction, but are concerned about use/abuse, consider implementing the following actions:

- Don't buy what you want to avoid — if it's not there it's less tempting
- Tell everyone around (or selected friends) to keep an eye on you
- Don't try to hide or lie if you fail — the only one you hurt and lie to is yourself
- Talk to your doctor

If your alcohol intake is relatively under control, but you want to moderate your consumption, intersperse water with every other drink. This will lessen the impact of the alcohol, you won't consume as much, and you will feel much better the next day, since water counteracts the dehydration that accompanies alcohol consumption.

If you feel you need support, attend an Alcoholics Anonymous (AA) meeting in your area. AA is a global organization dedicated to helping people recover in a non-judgmental, highly supportive environment.

Only you can determine if it's something you need to do or not — and there is no shame in seeking help if you need it.

☐ ERIC UPDATE

At the workshop: This is one of Eric's big issues, alcohol. When he was part of the work-group he didn't drink much alcohol, only a couple of beers during the week and a couple of glasses of wine on the weekends. The problems started about a year after he was promoted to the leadership position. Being required to attend more evening meetings, most of which ended with a dinner and, feeling more and more anxious, and a bit out of control, he noticed that a glass of wine would reduce the anxiety, 2 glasses were even better . . . and so on. He never felt drunk, and people around him praised his relaxed style which encouraged him to drink even more. Soon he began drinking more at home as well, despite the fact that Karin would ask him not to — he began to feel he needed alcohol to relax. It became a vicious cycle and he was really struggling with this issue. Frankly his harmful drinking was on the verge of addiction.

Task #1: We agreed that he would have every second glass of water at all dinners out.

Task #2: Include Karin in this commitment. The two would create a contract, for both to sign and agree to, that he would stop when she felt it was too much. Eric did not smoke, which is unusual for someone drinking this much, and he did not use any other drugs.

☐ End of Month 1

Update Task #2: Contract with Karin signed, and it was working well as it complemented the changes in sleep, food and physical activity. For him, even talking about the problem had helped.

☐ **End of Month 2**

Update Task #1: Consumption reduction continues.

☐ **End of Month 3**

He's actually beginning to feel like he's thinking more clearly, and he's not been hung over in a very long time. He's feeling lucky — like he dodged a bullet.

☐ **End of Month 4**

Feeling even better, and anxiety levels are decreasing substantially.

☐ **End of Month 5**

Feeling great and anxiety levels are at an all-time low.

☐ **End of Month 6**

Alcohol is no longer an issue. He is well aware that he was close to crossing the dangerous line into addiction, and he's thankful he's kicked it.

CHAPTER 3

Happiness at Work: Can You Feel It?

"Success is not the key to happiness. Happiness is the key to success. If you love what you are doing, you will be successful."

— Herman Cain

WE SPEND an average of eight hours a day, five days a week, for approximately 45 years at work. That's one-third of our life! And if you're a business leader, you most likely spend more. So what do you think about work? Do you hate Monday mornings with a passion? Do you merely "survive" the work week — anxiously anticipating time off on the weekend?

Perhaps the bigger question here is *why* do you work? Is it for the money? The social environment? Because you like the content and tasks involved in your current job and you want to do it well?

Unfortunately, too many people work because they have to, not because they want to. The problem is, if you don't enjoy your job, you probably won't be effective or do a good job. When you don't perform at your best, you begin to self-criticize, and a vicious cycle has begun. Hate the work, don't do the work, decide that for some reason, it's your fault initially — but then move to blaming the job, perhaps even your boss or colleagues, for the fact that you hate your job. Like I said, it's a vicious cycle.

Too much time in this cycle, can lead to serious illness (refer to the section on stress in the last chapter.) We now know what this type of situation can do to the body. Even if you love your job, and are relatively happy, you've picked up this book because you're feeling burnt out, stressed out, or concerned about the direction you're headed so something needs to change.

So how do we stop the cycle? It's easier than you think. It's time to take a step back, and discover why you're doing what you're doing. You can start by asking a few simple questions:

- Why do I work?
- Do I go to work with energy, anticipation and joy?
- Do I like my colleagues?
- Why did I accept this job in the first place?

If you dive deep, and answer these questions honestly, you will come to one of two conclusions. This job is for me, or this job is not for me.

If it's for you — it's time to get back on track to make it fun again. If it's not for you — it's time to look for a different path. I know this is no easy feat, but doing nothing will get you nowhere. Take a look at the following exercise. It's time to create a positive/negative — or **Plus/Minus list**. It helps to see everything on paper when you're in the process of making a big decision. (For a sample, and downloadable form, see Appendix F.)

Regardless of your decision to stay, or to take a different path, we can change the way we think about happiness at work. It's not necessarily job satisfaction (which has no correlation to doing good work), or the amount of money you make, or your beautiful office, etc. It's about how you *feel* about the work itself.

Basically, there are two fundamental requirements to being happy at work (and elsewhere too):

1. To create meaningful results. To make a difference for someone else. And to tell others when they have done something good.
2. To have solid, healthy, work relationships and a healthy work environment (Real relationships where you look into each other's eyes and say good morning and say something nice when you meet.)

It may sound odd to you to hear that you should look your colleagues in the eyes and smile, but it's a biological fact that we mirror each other's facial expressions. Grumpy, angry, sad, happy, joyful, etc. — these emotions are reflected back to us. And you won't be surprised to hear there are physiological benefits to smiling — that something this simple can have huge benefits. When people smile at each other, oxytocin — a powerful hormone that induces bonding and connection between people — is released. This release can actually break down social barriers, induce feelings of optimism, increase self-esteem, build trust, and create a general calm feeling for the people involved. Pretty amazing, right? And a happy workplace is a productive workplace and can generate great success for all — management, internal teams, clients, etc. It's a win-win situation.

In addition to the relationship factor, the work environment should be structured to promote and create efficiency — good structure actually creates freedom and ease in the workplace, which obviously helps us avoid stress, burn out and even prevents illness from occurring.

I use a **Systematic Work Environment Policy** for my clients' companies, offices or departments. (For a sample, and downloadable form, see Appendix G.)

Tailor this template to suit the needs of your place of business, and then address one issue at the time, as it relates to your structure. Similar to the Walk & Talk meetings, this may seem more time consuming at first, but if you have a system in place, and everyone is on board — knowing exactly where they stand and what their role is — it increases efficiency tremendously.

☐ ERIC UPDATE

At the workshop: Eric was the perfect IT-technician — you might say born into it since he began at such a young age. It was less about learning and more about something engrained in him. Many opportunities were given to him as a result — an excellent higher education, and ultimately, a high paying job. For ten years, he loved his job and was very happy at work, and he was flattered when he was promoted at the ten year mark.

The first couple of years were ok, although he felt increasingly isolated from his former co-workers. He did have five others in parallel positions, but he envied them because he thought they were handling the job much better — and he believe they thought so as well.

Then his department began losing money, and he covered it well so no one suspected it was as bad as it was. Then everything began to spiral downward — he felt he'd failed at his job and was digging his own grave risking not only his job, but his health and his family.

At the session, I asked him this critical question: Do you want this job?

Task #1: I asked him to create a positive/negative check list about his current position. It wasn't time to make a decision, since he was "in the throes" so to speak, but he needed to begin to reflect on the issue.

☐ **End of Month 1**

Update Task #1: At this point he had more negatives than positives on the list.

☐ **End of Month 2**

Update Task #1: He's now found some more positive aspects to add to the list, and he's discussed the future with his boss, who has agreed to let the issue be open for a while.

☐ **End of Months 3 and 4**

The positive side of the list continues to grow.

☐ **End of Month 5**

Things were really turning around at this point. He'd had another discussion with his boss, the department was getting back on its feet, and he was beginning to see a bright future at the company.

☐ **End of Month 6**

Everything was finally coming together. The company had utilized the Systematic Work Environment program to facilitate more effective operations, and to keep the employees happy at work leading to better performance. Although it was going to take a couple of years to implement, Eric earned accolades from the CEO for putting this structure in place.

CHAPTER 4

How Important is Money?

"If great truth does not enter into our relation to money, it cannot enter our lives."

— Jacob Needleman

THERE ARE so many conflicting clichés about money. "Money makes the world go around," "Money can't buy you happiness," "A penny saved, is a penny earned," "Easy come — easy go," and so on.

So how do you feel about money? Most people when asked this question respond either with raised eyebrows, a blank start, or an uncomfortable laugh. "What do you mean, how do I feel about money? It is what it is — it's money. It's a necessity — it pays my mortgage, my car note, the kids' school, food, etc., etc., etc." Here's the deal — money is more than that — it's not just about numbers, what you can buy, how much you make, the things you have — everyone has feelings attached to it. And the truth is, once you have enough to cover your basic needs, food, shelter, clothing and a few personal things, it's no longer a necessity.

This is a tough concept for most people to grasp. "The more money you have the better off you are, right? Money buys me the freedom to live on my own terms — and worrying about not having enough can literally make you ill." The truth is, no matter how much money people have, many worry themselves sick about not having enough. And it's not that they don't have enough, it's that they're afraid to look at their financial situation as it stands, whatever it may be, with open eyes. "If I don't see it, it doesn't exist." And business leaders have double this trouble — they often have two budgets to worry about — their own and the company's.

So guess what the first step is in regaining control of your finances? That's right! Write it all down. All of it. Write down your monthly income, and all expenses in a **Cash Flow Chart**. (It's important to note here that when I ask my clients to engage in this exercise, there's a huge discrepancy in what they *think* about their financial situation, and how it *really is*.) This exercise is very important to complete — it will show you where you really are in terms of your finances, relieving a lot of fear and anxiety. (For a sample, and downloadable form, see Appendix H.)

The biggest issue I run into here, it that most of my clients worry incessantly about not having enough money, but behave as if they have more than enough. Some even overspend due to the anxiety created by the very fact that they think they don't have enough, when in reality, they have no idea how much money they actually do have. And a further dimension is although people say they don't have enough money for critical things like health care, they do have the *latest and greatest gadgets in phones, iPads, etc. Seem convoluted? There's a reason for that.* Most people do not like to talk about money . . . it's taboo in many societies, and we have deeply ingrained, yet often unspoken, attitudes about it: "Rich people are greedy," "Poor people are not very intelligent," "Don't brag about having a lot of money," etc.

Think about what your parents told you about money, and it's likely you believe and act the same. Were you constantly told "We can't afford that?" or "There's not enough," or the opposite, "The world is your oyster!" Whatever messages you received as a child about money, are most likely still with you and form the basis of your attitudes and dealings with money today.

We can change that simply by taking control and creating an **Annual** family/private **Budget**. (For a sample, and downloadable form, see Appendix I.)

Of course businesses always have budgets — but they're not always effective or accurate. If you have a gut feeling that things are not in order, there's only one thing to do — face the real facts, and take action. Be honest and open with your boss (or partner) and deal with the situation as soon as possible. It's the only way to alleviate any accompanying anxiety, and in most situations, any issues are completely resolvable if both parties are willing to have the conversation and commit to the actions required to remedy the situation.

☐ ERIC UPDATE

At the workshop: Eric is not a poor man, he's considered upper middle class by Swedish standards. He and Karin share all finances, but neither is interested in creating a budget. Raised in a family with limited resources, money was never discussed. Not only was it not discussed, but it was "ugly" to be rich ("rich people are greedy" kind of thinking) so it was considered not appropriate to discuss. Eric and Karin's children are brought up knowing there's a limited amount of money.

At the first meeting, it's apparent that Eric is in the dark about his finances — both at home and at work. Karin manages the home budget, and he's comfortable with that, even though he used to be in charge.

His budget at work is in trouble, however. Last year turnaround was only 13 million SEK (1.6 million USD) when it should have been 25 million SEK (3.6 million USD). Department efficacy has almost decreased to half — it's close to catastrophic — and they've lost a few long-term clients. He's under so much pressure he feels like he can't even remember how to count anymore. Of course he's kept this all hidden for some time, and even has told half-truths at meetings, so much so he's even begun to believe it himself. Needless to say, he is relieved to lay it all out on the table. It's been quite a heavy burden to carry.

Task #1: Meet with his boss and deal upfront and directly with the issue.

☐ **End of Month 1**

Update Task #1: As expected, his boss was aware of the problem, but not the extent of the problem. For now, budget responsibilities were transferred to another team member — both agreed this would be best, and accountant was brought in to review where they were, and advice on next steps. This actually was quite a relief for Eric.

☐ **End of Month 2**

The accountant regained control of the numbers and has got control of the numbers and a few money leaks have been plugged.

☐ **End of Months 3 and 4**

No changes.

☐ End of Month 5

The company conducted a seminar about integrity where they discussed making the right choices, helping each other out, and being generally kind toward one another. They also discussed budgets and transparency. After the workshop, many of the others came to Eric to give him support. This was the first time in a long while that Eric felt like he was finding his old self again. At this stage, it was critical that people supported him.

☐ End of Month 6

Eric now has full control of the department budget again. Revenue is still not back up to the desired level, but it's steadily increasing. Also, as a result of the past situation, the company has developed an "early warning" system to head off any potential future problems early in the game. The entire team is grateful as it now feels more safe and secure for everyone. And none of it would have taken place, if he hadn't "broken down."

CHAPTER 5

Can You Relate?

"Man is by nature a social animal; an individual who is unsocial naturally and not accidentally is either beneath our notice or more than human. Society is something that precedes the individual. Anyone who either cannot lead the common life or is so self-sufficient as not to need to, and therefore does not partake of society, is either a beast or a god."

— *Aristotle,* Politics

W E'RE SOCIAL BEINGS — "pack animals" so to speak. To a certain extent, this makes life easier. We can help each other out — achieve more together. We're all driven to be part of a bigger picture — to belong to a group. At the same time, however, we're individuals with our own dreams and wishes, our own needs and wants, behaviors, etc. And these differences can be celebrated and appreciated, or they can cause tension and strife. As we know, tense external situations can create internal conflicts when people find themselves part of a group, or work situation, that doesn't nourish or support their needs and desires. It's true that we don't have to "like" everyone we meet, but we must treat them with respect. Disrespect among colleagues will damage the workplace environment in no time at all.

So how do we deal with this? We must take complete responsibility for ourselves. If we're in a work situation that we feel is unsupportive — or even toxic — we still must treat people with respect, but decide to move on. It's the same for our personal relationships. Take a long look at the "groups" with who you are currently involved (family, friends, business partners, colleagues, acquaintances, etc.) and ask yourself the following:

- What do I think about these people/this person?
- How do I feel when I'm with them? Do I feel energized and happy? Or do I feel drained and stressed, or depressed?
- Do I spend time with them because I think I have to, or because I want to?

Then flip the coin . . .
- What do they think about me? Do I even know?
- How do they feel when they're with me?
- How would I want them to see me? And so on . . .

This process requires quite a bit of introspection. Take a long hard look at your close network, your extended network, and your family relationships. It's amazing what you will find when you really look at these relationships, and how they impact your day-to-day life. And there are times when it's simply better to let go of a relationship that constantly drains your energy. It may seem harsh at first, but soon you will realize it's not harsh at all — just a simple fact that your differences prevent a long-term relationship so it's healthiest for both to move on. Even if you can't literally "let go" or move on, as happens with colleagues or sometimes even extended family, you can change your thoughts and feelings — create a critical distance emotionally — which will protect you from being robbed of your own energy and happiness.

It's really important for people to have at least one or two close connections with people — it keeps us sane. But in terms of the networks we are a part of, the organizations we join, etc — it's up to you. Big, small, many, few — you choose what works best for you.

At this point, it might be helpful to refer to the Ensize communication map. Try to pinpoint where you think the people close to you are on the map. And then see them through your "map perspective." At the very least, it will help you understand why they behave the way they do — even if you aren't particularly fond of a person, this might help you better understand where they're coming from, and how they relate to others, which can alleviate a little tension.

I use the following Mindmap to help clients determine where they want to be in this spectrum.

Network Mind Map

☐ ERIC UPDATE

At the workshop: When we first meet, Eric´s network is in pieces. He feels all alone in the world and thinks nobody likes him, not even his wife Karin. The family used to have informal dinners with friends, but that hasn't happened in over a year.

At work, he feels rejected both because he thinks they are critical of his performance, and his team does not like working for him. It's why he's hiding at work.

The truth is, though, that he's not letting them into his world. He often gets home late after client dinners (with too much alcohol). And even though people tell him good things, he finds it hard to believe, and thinks they may be making fun of him, or patronizing him. He feels bad about himself, so he drinks more.

Life is sad!

Well, this is the picture as he sees it.

Task #1: Make a mindmap of his network.

☐ End of Month 1

Update Task #1: He's found eight different groups in his network. Some of them may be divided into smaller sub-groups too.

- Family
- Long-term friends from childhood and youth
- Newer family friends
- Neighbors
- Workmates
- Business relations
- Children's parents etc
- "Odds and ends" (his term)

New Task #2: Choose 10–15 people he would like to keep close.

☐ End of Month 2

Update Task #2: We review his list of 14 people — taken from the different groups listed in the first task.

New Task #3: Connect, and let these people know they are important to him. (He finds this a challenge, but promises to try.)

☐ End of Month 3

Update Task #3: He's connected with half his list and it's been such a good experience, he sees the ultimate benefit. He also has begun to loosen up a bit and use "the smile, and hello, method" again in relationships — both existing and new.

☐ End of Month 4

Update Task #3: He's connected with all 14 on his list, and has even added a couple more.

New Task #4: Identify people he needs to separate from — those who may drain his energy, or have a negative influence.

☐ End of Month 5

Update Task #4: He found 5 individuals on this list. Two were important work relationships, but the other three were distant connections he could let go. The strategy we develop at work is from him to be polite, and keep the conversation focused on work, changing it back if it begins to drift. And, if it becomes too difficult, he will ask to reschedule the meetings to a later date so has some time to think about the issue.

☐ End of Month 6

Update Task #4: He's had three situations last month where he had to use the "escape plan." It worked very well, and at the next meeting he was prepared to protect himself from the energy drain.

Since he's been feeling so much better over all, he's also had much more lively contact with his entire network. It's crystal clear how important this inner circle of friends is to him, as well as the people who aren't as close, but that he still enjoys being around.

Now that he's back on track with his existing relationships, he's feeling much more joy about meeting new people. And, with the new communication tools we've worked on together, his conversations with new people are different, certainly not stressful and always without judgment. This is working well for him in both his personal and professional life — he's expanding his professional network, and his sales meetings are much more productive.

CHAPTER **6**

Come a Little Closer

*"You can close your eyes to things you don't want to see, but you
can't close your heart to the things you don't want to feel."*

— Unknown

D O YOU REMEMBER your first really close contact? Probably not
because you get that when you are a newborn. Or at least should
get. The correlation between high infant rate mortality among babies
raised in orphanages is well established. During, the most frequent
bombing of London in World War 2, many newborns were sent
to "nurseries" in the countryside — far away from the active war.
They were supposed to be safer there. The physical standard was
good, but they were understaffed; the babies got what they needed
such as food and clean diapers but no time for play and cuddling.
Despite these fairly good conditions, many babies died. A closer look
revealed that most of the babies who had died were placed in the
far corners — only looked at periodically, and cuddled at the time
set for them. Nobody passed their bed at any other time. The babies
with beds closest to the nurse's office lived. Many people passed by
during the day and they received more attention, smiles and loving

caresses. This historical situation taught us a lot. It brought home the fact that we need much more than food and protection to survive.

Furthermore, it is the early bonds that establish our ability to trust later in life — and impact how we are in our close relationships. We want to be seen and heard. When people do not feel seen and heard, they often seek attention — in any form. Think of the teen who is ignored. He drives down your street one day in the car he's been working so diligently to repair, saying "hey, notice me . . ." He's quiet, at first, but as he is repeatedly ignored, the engine gets louder, the wave turns to a yell, until one day he is racing down the street at high speed, engine roaring, yelling out the window, until he finally crashes and takes out a tree in the neighbor's yard.

It's essential for every human being to be noticed:

- ◆ to be positively acknowledged for being who you are (Eric is a good person); and
- ◆ to be positively acknowledged for the things you do (Eric is doing a good job).

In addition to being noticed, people need love and physical contact — caressing — and physical intimacy — sex. Skin contact and caressing releases "feel good" hormones. That's why we like to hold hands, give hugs and other close contacts when we meet. Physical intimacy is the ultimate way of close contact and it includes one of our strongest drives, libido, to reproduce ourselves. Unfortunately, stress and lack of sleep play a major role in reduced libido. It becomes a chore, or even a problem, instead of something to enjoy. Here's how it works. The marriage becomes like another business. You deal with your children and your partner in front of the television with a laptop on your knee as if you're dealing with your employees. By the time you're ready to even consider thinking about intimacy, the "right feeling" isn't there, so you both drift into sleep, night after night. But you stick your head in the sand, and hope it will pass, which it doesn't. And one day, you look at the person next to you, and wonder who they even are. After all, it's become more and more like a business relationship over time — each does his/her part — just do what has to be done — no discussions, no private talks, and no everyday intimacy. There may be some hasty sex every second week just because it "should" be, but there's no real intimacy — you may even be thinking about the budget at work during sex, or even worse using it to take out aggression and frustration.

The problem is exacerbated by the "picture" we want to create — the ever-happy, successful, "has-it-all" leader. But it's not the reality. The amount of emotional conflict present is tremendous — there is seemingly no possible way, really, to have it all. According to a survey among 1428 leaders done by the magazine "Chef" in Sweden only 20 % of business leaders feel they still have enough time for the partner and family after becoming a boss — due to problems at work and long work hours. Forty-five percent say their sex life has decreased.

Sounds hopeless, doesn't it? It's not! You *can* find balance between work and home, but you must choose to do it. Prioritize. It won't happen on its own.

If you value your relationship with your partner — and like your job — you have to think things over and make active choices. It *is* possible to have both if you work on it.

So, take **Intimacy Inventory**. Every leader with love problems should sit down and really look at their life — as it is now, not what they hope it to be. How important is my relationship? How do I want to live my life? What do I need to do to get there? Decide what kind of human being you want to be. What, exactly are your priorities? Write the answers on a piece of paper — it will make them more real and graspable. (For a sample, and downloadable form, see Appendix J.)

That being said, you must, at some point, be able to turn the phone off and take the discussion with your partner!

☐ ERIC UPDATE

At the workshop: Initially, Eric is very uncomfortable discussing this issue. He's embarrassed to admit that not only is Karin putting him off, she's shared that she feels the intimacy in their relationship is gone — that he's just using her for sex. As he begins to feel more comfortable, the floodgates open, and he's talking up a storm. (It's amazing what comes out when people finally talk about something they feel they've been hiding for a very long time.)

Task #1: We discuss ways he can bring romance and love back to his relationship: buying flowers, date nights with dinner and a movie or simply staying at home and talking. He decides to let her know, however he can, that he wants their loving relationship back.

☐ End of Month 1

Update Task #1: It took him two weeks to talk with Karin since he was struggling with the right approach, but he finally got it right. After an hour-long conversation, they agreed to work together to bring the warmth and love back because they wanted the relationship to last.

☐ End of Month 2

Update Task #1: Karin still felt he was working too much and that he wasn't trying hard enough. From his perspective, although he chose not to argue about it, she was being unfair — he felt he was working diligently on all levels to get his good life back. He chose not to argue the point, but ended up leaving a lot to avoid having to think about it.

☐ End of Month 3

Things were getting better. There were less arguments, and he began keeping her in the loop on when he had business dinners so she didn't feel ignored.

☐ End of Month 4

As Eric was finding a happier, gentler self, the relationship began to rejuvenate, and trust was being restored.

☐ End of Month 6

Update Task #1: Karin came along to our final, personal meeting. She thanked me for helping return the love of her life to her, and for helping the relationship become even stronger. What easily could have ended in divorce, had become a fulfilling relationship for both.

CHAPTER 7

Free Time Rests Your Brain!

"We do not quit playing because we grow old,
we grow old because we quit playing."

— *Oliver Wendell Homes*

G O HAVE SOME FUN! People have very different views on free time, and play. But it really doesn't matter — just *know* what it is for you, and *do it*! It's fine to be committed to work, but our minds need time to recover, and our bodies need to move.

It's been said that time is the great equalizer — meaning that it's the only thing in life where we all have the same amount — 24 hours a day. Most business leaders work much longer than eight hours per day. And it's ok to work long hours when necessary — just be sure it's necessary. At some point, we reach what is called "the law of diminished returns." Meaning that we think we're accomplishing more by putting in tons of hours, staying late, giving up weekends, etc., but in fact our minds are exhausted so it takes longer to accomplish tasks than it would if we were well rested and energized.

Creating a Time Circle is a good tool to use to see how you're using your time. It's not very practical to take an overview of a single

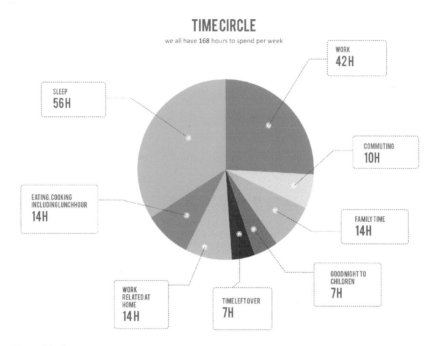

TIME CIRCLE
we all have **168** hours to spend per week

WORK
42H

COMMUTING
10H

FAMILY TIME
14H

GOOD NIGHT TO
CHILDREN
7H

TIME LEFT OVER
7H

WORK
RELATED AT
HOME
14H

EATING, COOKING
INCLUDING LUNCH HOUR
14H

SLEEP
56H

Time Circle

day because the days may vary. We can take a general snapshot of the week, however, to see where we're spending our time.

Resting your brain, however, does not mean lying on the couch. It can mean that as well but not for too long. Rest of mind is taking a break from your usual work responsibilities and tasks, and focusing on something entirely different — without pressure. Something you find fun, engaging, stimulating, relaxing, etc.

Maybe it's been so long since you've had free time, you've forgotten what you like to do outside of work. If you can't remember, think about trying something new: photography, painting, wood craft, textile work, reading, writing, going to opera/theater/movies, stamp collecting, walks in the forest, hiking, biking, skiing — the list is endless and the choice is yours.

Here's an exercise to help you remember, or find something new. Make a list of 10 things you used to enjoy doing, do or always wanted to do. When you're done, ask yourself how you feel about each of them, and add a plus by the ones that seem great, and a minus by the ones that don't appeal to as much. Then go for it!

You may be asking, what does any of this have to do with health? It's a big piece of the puzzle in terms of your well-being. It's kind of like "cross-training" your brain. When you use all parts, each individual part begins to work better. Take a look at the following example.

"I had a client once whom I initially also sent to the health care center because he was complaining of fatigue and I felt it was more than stress. He needed a real medical checkup. He owned a 15-car taxi company, and he was the administrator and driver all rolled into one. He literally worked day and night. It was easy to understand he was tired. He was heavily overweight and blood tests results demonstrated skyrocketing cholesterol and he was close to getting diabetes. This man was really at risk.

We started by discussing the importance of sleep and healthy food choices. (He never slept, and he ate junk food to stay awake while he drove taxi at night.) And he was sitting still all day in the office and all night in the taxi car. He changed the schedule for all drivers and managed to get himself out of the system at nights. Within a few weeks, and some good sleep, he was motivated to discuss more changes. He told me he had always wanted to write a book about his life as a taxi driver and all of the fantastic stories he'd heard, and the interesting people he'd met, but "everybody" in his circle had always been negative so he'd tucked the dream away and worked even more.

Here's what happened: He was still very overweight and fought the idea of keeping a food diary, so we created an alternate exercise. He agreed to decide what he would write about, take a brisk 30-minute walk, and then write whatever came to his mind. The walk triggered his thinking and he wrote for 3+ minutes when he got home.

I met him again about 2 months later. He'd lost some weight, his blood sugar level was normal, cholesterol was lower, and best of all he was happy. He had hired administrative help for the business, his book was half way done (from his point of view) and he was about to start at a gym now that he had energy enough to go there. He said he had his life back."

This short story demonstrates that when you engage in a different activity, one where there's no pressure to perform, it can open up the possibility of even greater performance when you return to the tasks at hand. It also shows the importance of moving the body — it can literally change your life!

☐ ERIC UPDATE

At the workshop: At the first meeting, Eric hadn't had any time off for a long time. That didn't mean he was working all the time, he was just misusing his time because there was no organization, or real awareness — time just flew by. He did have 1 or 2 nights out with clients and he did work late at least 2 more nights. The evenings he spent at home he just watched television since he had no energy left and Karin and he had stopped talking.

He used to like soccer when he was younger, and he said he enjoyed taking walks in the woods. So, since they live close to a forest/recreation area with trails and lights, he committed to start walking in there — getting exercise and doing something he enjoyed. He'd also been thinking about drawing or woodworking as hobbies.

(Not that this was the time to start, but it was good to shed light on something of interest down the road.) One of his best friends from the early days had always told Eric that woodworking was a lifeline — a great way to relax the mind.

We started to do a Time Circle, but didn't complete it since he wanted to spend a little more time thinking about it — so, it was **Task #1** for the next call.

☐ End of Month 1

Update Task #1: The Time Circle indicated he had about seven free hours per week to do whatever he enjoyed. He still couldn't see them at this point, though, since his life was still pretty disorganized. And, he'd come across an ad about an illustration course for technicians he was enthused about (earlier he would never have noticed this ad, but now it just flashed right in front of him). It was exactly what he wanted and it began in two months. He still felt a bit overwhelmed so he had not sent in the application yet.

New Task #2: Send in application.

☐ End of Month 2

Update Task #2: He'd sent the application in and was feeling pretty good about it.

☐ End of Month 3

He'd received a list for things to buy before the course and he was very excited about it.

New Task #3: Get those things.

☐ End of Month 4

Update Task #3: The course had started and he'd been there twice. The teacher noted the good work he was doing, and he became absolutely absorbed at the workshops. He was enjoying it so much, it began to take a little too much of his time, so we discussed how he could maneuver time by being more efficient at work.

☐ End of Month 5

With four weeks of the workshops left, he was still doing great and enjoying the experience, but it wasn't as high a priority.

☐ End of Month 6

When he looks at all drawings he's produced, it's clear that this experience has been soul nurturing. The course is complete, but he plans to keep it up at home.

CHAPTER 8

Where Do You Belong?

"People further down the social ladder usually run at least twice the risk of serious illness and premature death of those near the top."

— *World Health Organization (WHO)*

WHERE YOU LIVE, how you feel about where you live and your social status (and how you perceive it) impacts your health and your longevity. In fact, according to epidemiologist, Michael Marmot, "You probably didn't realize that when you graduated from college you increased your lifespan, or that your colleague who has a master's degree is more likely to live a longer and healthier life. Seemingly small social differences in education, job title, income, even the size of your house or apartment have a profound impact on your health." (The Status Syndrome: How Social Standing Affects Our Health and Longevity. 2004.)

His research also found that "relative position" also matters. In other words, people who feel they live above the minimum resources required, as compared to others, have better health. Most people live alongside those with similar resources — they have about the same living standards. But, there's always a slight difference — they may have about the same amount of money, but one sits higher on the social scale — and that person tends to live longer and suffer less disease. A good example of this is the fact that Oscar-winning actors live an average of four years longer than those actors who were just nominated.

This is astounding news! How can it be that a small difference in education or a small difference in living area (3 vs. 4 room apartment) can influence longevity? The answer is that above a certain lowest level of material living standard — or basic needs (e.g. food, shelter, etc.) — another kind of wellbeing is playing a key role in our overall health and welfare. Research seems to show that the more autonomous people are — the more control they have over their own situation — coupled with healthy and full social engagement is critical part of the health puzzle.

Though surprising, it seems like a simple concept. But it's quite complicated. It's not only the economic situation itself, but what the cost has been to "arrive," and how people feel about it. We all know there can be a big downside to being at the top. Stress is multiplied and many "burn the candle at both ends," not being able to find time to take care of their health, or to get away from the office to relax or play. Obviously this creates health issues.

And then there's the "envy" factor. Even in the same socioeconomic environment, people tend to think the "grass is always greener" on the other side. It's been my experience that it's not "greener," it's just a different shade of green. In any event, these feelings can create conflict both internally and externally.

So the physical environment issue has at least two dimensions — The socio-economic issue and the envy part. Both may have deep impact on your health, and the best way to deal with is, as usual, to talk about it!

There's another critical piece of the puzzle when we're talking about the physical environment we live in. Climate, opportunities for you or your spouse, neighborhood relationships, amount of sun or not, transportation, proximity to cultural events, and more — all of these things impact our perceived quality of life, and therefore, our overall health and well-being. "Go where you grow," instead of "bloom where you're planted."

When I have my clients work with this piece of the health issue, I ask them to write down what they think about where they live, their friendship with neighbors, nature, commute time to work, the cost of commuting, and anything else they find relevant to living where they live in a **Pros and Cons List**. The discussion most often is very interesting as this exercise brings up things they've never thought about before, or didn't realize. (For a sample, and downloadable form, see Appendix K.)

I once had a client who always felt "small" whenever he ran into a specific neighbor. At first he couldn't explain why — but after some reflection, he remembered this neighbor commenting on his garden, stating that he did not like the way it was maintained, and that it was a mess! (The neighbor's garden was in perfect order so it made my client fear he was being judged — that he wasn't good enough. And he was a powerful, successful businessman.) Here's the rub. When confronted, the neighbor had not given his statement a second thought — it had been years ago! So my client was holding onto something that he could have let go of a long time ago. Today they are best friends and the man next door often helps my client in the garden since he is retired and he just loves gardening.

I tell you this story because something truly fascinating happened as a result of my client's resolution of this issue. His confidence was boosted, so he also began taking risks in his business that generated huge results. Big wins for him on many levels. It also underscores the fact that health is not just about food, physical activity, sleep, or stress. It's also about how we face and address issues in our lives, and how we problem solve. It really is a complex puzzle.

☐ ERIC UPDATE

At the workshop: Eric lives in a small town of 15,000 souls. It's a "sleepy" little town, where most people commute to their job in a bigger city which is 20 minutes away. It's mostly single family homes, and the areas with apartments are where the "poor" live.

Eric lives in a relatively wealthy area with fairly big houses and nice gardens — although neither he, nor Karin cares to garden so their garden is like a wild grown area. The house also is a bit big for them, and between their hectic work schedule and raising their children, they rarely have time to enjoy it. Their children attend a school nearby and are happy there. They have many friends in the area.

Although he and Karin had discussed moving to the city to be closer to work, they really haven't been talking much lately, so we agree to table this issue at this point as there's work to do in other areas.

☐ Months 1–4

This is almost a non-issue as Eric is dealing other issues.

☐ End of Month 5

By this time, Eric's most pressing issues are getting in order and he brings this up again. (The issue resurfaced as one of the children's friends is moving to Stockholm.) He brings it up, because now that it's back on the table, the whole family had different ideas on about the pros and cons of a potential move.

Task #1: Make a pros and cons list. (Each family member)

☐ End of Month 6

Update Task #1: Key pros for staying include:

+ They live in a respected area.
+ Good environment.
+ The children love the neighborhood, their school and friends.
+ It's a status symbol (what would people say if they leave this "luxurious" life? Would they look down on them? This is a big fear for Eric — it's very important for him to be seen as a powerful, successful man.)

Key cons for staying include:

+ There's a lot of time spent in the car.
+ Although the house is big, they don't spend a lot of time there, and they feel they don't have time for household and garden activities (both would like to live differently, but they feel like it's such a big thing to change.)

It's obvious that it's not the time to make this critical decision, so we discuss another task.

New Task #2: Since their house is large, they've accumulated a lot of stuff over the years. Making a move at the moment would be tough. Both he and Karin agree that for at least one hour, each weekend, they will sort out the basement, garage, bookshelves, cupboards, drawers, closets and any other place where things hide. (That's 52 hours over a year — plenty of time to get things done. The task includes finding "the place" for everything they want to keep, and to get rid of the rest. Although he fights this at first, saying there isn't enough time, we discuss that by simply breaking down the task into more manageable pieces, much can be accomplished in a year.

Summary

S O, NOW YOU'VE SEEN how the Wheel of Life works. And you met Eric, and watched how he worked on each of the pieces, and implemented substantive changes over a six month period of time. (In the scheme of things, that's not very long.) His work throughout the process also demonstrates that the pieces may be separate, but there's spill over into all areas — if you address issues facing you in one area, they can impact issues in other areas. It's all connected — each piece contributes to the larger puzzle.

When we first met, Eric's overall health was at risk — he was facing some very serious challenges, and he was scared. His blood pressure was high, and he was getting closer to developing diabetes — what some call "the silent killer." He also was overweight, and at an increased risk of heart attack or stroke. Instead of focusing on the threat, together we worked on developing new, healthy habits, and slowly, but surely, he lost weight, and his lab results indicated a substantial decrease in all of the areas where he was at risk. As I've mentioned — change is never a "do it, and done with it" deal — it's a process. My program is not about quick-fixes, it's about making life changes that have a positive impact on our overall health and wellbeing in all areas of our lives. And, as you've seen, it doesn't have to be overwhelming. Even the smallest of initial steps can lead to bigger steps, and, ultimately, much better outcomes.

I think witnessing Eric's process also shows that transparency and openness are key factors to feeling good. We must face the facts in all situations in life — even when it seems difficult. In the long run, it alleviates anxiety, and can pave the way for easier problem-solving/problem prevention in the future.

The big bonus for Eric was that the impact of his work not only benefitted him and his family, it extended to his work environment as well. Since he's returned to being a confident, happy leader, and he shared his growth experience and the tools necessary to achieve that growth, his entire department has become more connected and effective. It will be an honor to walk another year with him as he continues his good work and amazing growth.

Here's to your good health!

Appendix A
Sleep Diary

Upon arising. Fill in this section in the morning when you wake up.

Sleeping habits	Monday/ Tuesday	Tuesday/ Wednesday	Wednesday/ Thursday	Thursday/ Friday	Friday/ Saturday	Saturday/ Sunday	Sunday/ Monday
Bed Time							
Time you woke up							
How long it took you to fall asleep							
How many times did you wake up during the night?							
How many hours/minutes sleep did you get?							
Use of sleeping pills?							
Amount of coffee before bedtime							

To download and print a copy, go to www.chaostocalm.me/appendix

Sleeping habits	Monday/ Tuesday	Tuesday/ Wednesday	Wednesday/ Thursday	Thursday/ Friday	Friday/ Saturday	Saturday/ Sunday	Sunday/ Monday
Amount of alcohol before bedtime							
How was your sleep? 1. very bad 2. fairly bad 3. neutral 4. fairly good 5. very good							

Just before going to bed: How was your day?
1 = not at all, 2 = a little, 3 = some, 4 = fairly much, 5 = much

This part shows your daytime problems	Monday	Tuesday	Wednesdayy	Thursday	Friday	Saturday	Sunday
Tired							
Concentration problems							
Stressed							
Memory problems							
Irritated							
Depressed							
Physical pain							

To download and print a copy, go to www.chaostocalm.me/appendix

Appendix B
Diet Diary

Record *everything* you eat during each day of the week.

Dates	Breakfast	Lunch	Dinner	Snacks
Monday				
Tuesday				
Wednesday				
Thursday				
Friday				
Saturday				
Sunday				

To download and print a copy, go to www.chaostocalm.me/appendix

Appendix C
Physical Activity Diary

Fill in only what you *have* done, not what you want or hope to do.

Date	Activity	How many?	Time Spent/Duration
Jan 3	*Ex: Sit ups*	*15*	*5 minutes*

To download and print a copy, go to www.chaostocalm.me/appendix

Appendix D
Stress Journal

Dates	Activity that provokes stress and for how long? (describe what happens in your body)	Level 0–10
Monday	*Ex: Traffic jam on way to work — 30 minutes late — didn't settle down until coffee break at 10am.*	*8*
	Didn't get to sit down to eat lunch because I was running behind. Affected the entire afternoon.	*6*
Tuesday		
Wednesday		
Thursday		
Friday		
Saturday		
Sunday		

To download and print a copy, go to www.chaostocalm.me/appendix

Appendix E
"Important/ Urgent Tool"

	Important	Not important
Urgent		
Not Urgent		

To download and print a copy, go to www.chaostocalm.me/appendix

Appendix F
Plus-Minus List

Job

Where do I want to work?	Current job		New job	
	pros	cons	pros	cons
Hours				
Salary				
Benefits				
Etc — fill in as many things as you can think of				

To download and print a copy, go to www.chaostocalm.me/appendix

Appendix G
Work Environment Policy

WE AGREE that *friendship* and *stimulating* work tasks are examples of important factors supporting the environment at our workplace. Our goal is to create a workplace where dangers and risks for illness due to work are recognized and effectively addressed. Consequently:

☐ We recognize and fix risks in our daily work.

☐ We follow up to ensure work environment rules are properly followed.

☐ We develop effective routines, aligned with the work environment, and properly divide responsibility of all tasks, making constant improvements in all parts.

☐ We regularly follow up to ensure that everybody has the knowledge, resources and power to make it possible to take personal responsibility for the work environment.

To download and print a copy, go to www.chaostocalm.me/appendix

☐ We examine the work environment at least once a year with the help of check lists in order to prevent injury and illness.

☐ We investigate illness, injuries and incidents to prevent repeating.

☐ We have regular work place meetings where we discuss the work place in general, including the work environment issues.

☐ We follow up on our work environment program at least once a year following a special agenda.

☐ We live up to the requirements of documentation and clarity.

Signature: _____ Date: _____

Dated and signed by the person responsible for work environment.

To download and print a copy, go to www.chaostocalm.me/appendix

Appendix H

Cash
Flow Chart

Month:

Date	Rent/ mortgage	Food	Hygiene	Clothes	Leisure	Other1	Other2	Income
1								
2								
3								
4								
5								
Etc								
31								
Sum								
Result = income − costs								

To download and print a copy, go to www.chaostocalm.me/appendix

Appendix I
Annual Budget

Note: Complete the Cash Flow Chart for one month to see your levels prior to completing the budget.

Incomes		Per month	Per year
Income 1			
Income 2			
Income 3			
Sum Incomes			
Costs			
Rent/mortgage			
Electricity, water, heating			
Food Consumables			
Clothes			
Hygiene			
Hobbies			

To download and print a copy, go to www.chaostocalm.me/appendix

Costs		Per month	Per year
Cigarettes Alcohol			
etc			
etc			
Sum Costs			
Incomes minus costs			

To download and print a copy, go to www.chaostocalm.me/appendix

Appendix J
Intimacy Inventory

So, take inventory. Describe things as they are now, not as you hope they will be.

How important is my relationship? How do I want to live my life? What do I need to do to get there? Decide what kind of human being I want to be. What, exactly are my priorities?

My priorities:

1 _____

2 _____

3 _____

My most important relations:

1 _____

2 _____

3 _____

To download and print a copy, go to www.chaostocalm.me/appendix

I want people to see me as _____

_____

_____

I want to be remembered for _____

_____

_____

Appendix K
Pros and Cons List

Where do you want to live?

	Pros	Cons
Stay	Ex: Good neighbors	Ex: House too big
Move	Ex: Shorter commute	Ex: Further away from family

To download and print a copy, go to www.chaostocalm.me/appendix